Quick & Easy
CHRISTMAS CAKES

ELAINE MACGREGOR

J. B. FAIRFAX

I would like to thank my husband, Stuart MacGregor, who has put all my half-formed words into English

Published by Merehurst Limited

Distributed by J. B. Fairfax Press Ltd
9 Trinity Centre, Park Farm Estate
Wellingborough, Northants

Text copyright © Elaine MacGregor 1993
Photography © Merehurst Limited 1993

ISBN 1-874567-55-7

Edited by Bridget Jones
Designed by Jo Tapper
Photography by Zul Mukhida
Colour separation by Scantrans, Singapore
Printed by Canale, Italy

NOTES ON USING THE RECIPES

For all recipes, quantities are given in metric, Imperial and cup measurements. Follow one set of measures only as they are not interchangeable. Standard 5ml teaspoons (tsp) and 15ml tablespoons (tbsp) are used. Australian readers, whose tablespoons measure 20ml, should adjust quantities accordingly. All spoon measures are assumed to be level unless otherwise stated.
Eggs are a standard size 3 (medium) unless otherwise stated.

CONTENTS

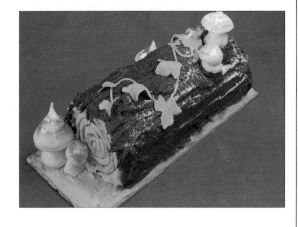

BASIC RECIPES

SWISS (JELLY) ROLL

3 large eggs
90g (3 oz/⅓ cup) caster (superfine) sugar
90g (3 oz/¼ cup) plain (all-purpose) flour,
sifted and left in a warm place
EQUIPMENT
30 x 20cm (12 x 8 inch) Swiss roll tin (jelly roll pan)
non-stick baking spray, non-stick paper or
teflon-coated baking sheet
clean tea-towel

❧ Preheat the oven to 230°C (450°F/Gas 8). Spray the tin (pan) with non-stick baking spray or grease and line it with non-stick paper or teflon-coated baking sheet.

❧ Put the eggs and sugar into the large mixing bowl and place this over a saucepan of hot water on low heat. Whisk the mixture by hand, preferably using a balloon whisk, until it thickens and becomes light and fluffy. The whisk should leave a trail over the surface as it is lifted. It takes about 10 minutes of whisking to achieve this consistency. Do not stop or the mixture will settle.

❧ Remove the bowl from the saucepan and gently fold in the flour. The mixture should resemble lightly whipped cream: if it is too thick, fold in a few drops of warm water. Pour the mixture into the prepared tin and spread it evenly. Bake for 8 – 10 minutes, until risen, golden and springy to the touch.

❧ Meanwhile, lay a sheet of non-stick paper on a dampened tea-towel and sprinkle with caster (superfine) sugar. Cut another sheet of non-stick paper just bigger than the tin. As soon as the cake is cooked, turn it out onto the sugared paper.

❧ Trim all the edges and make a shallow cut across the cake about 2.5cm (1 inch) from one narrow edge. This will allow the cake to roll more easily. The cake may be spread with jam (conserve) and must then be rolled immediately. Alternatively, lay the second sheet of paper on top of the cake and roll it up inside the cake. Use the tea-towel and sugared paper as a guide for lifting and rolling the cake, see page 27. When cool, the cake can be unrolled, the paper removed and a filling added.

Makes a 20cm (8 inch) long Swiss (jelly) roll

SPONGE CAKE

250g (8 oz/1 cup) butter or margarine
250g (8 oz/1¼ cups) caster (superfine) sugar
4 eggs, lightly beaten
250g (8 oz/2 cups) self-raising flour, sifted
EQUIPMENT
20cm (8 inch) round cake tin (pan)
non-stick baking spray, non-stick paper or
teflon-coated baking sheet

❧ Preheat the oven to 190°C (375°F/Gas 5). Grease and flour the tin (pan). Make sure the excess flour is knocked out of the tin. Alternatively, spray the tin with non-stick baking spray or line it with teflon-coated baking sheet.

❧ Cream the butter or margarine and sugar together until light and fluffy. Gradually add the eggs and mix well, adding a spoonful of the flour. Fold in the flour (do not beat it in) and turn the mixture into the prepared tin.

❧ Bake for about 45 minutes or until a skewer inserted into the centre of the cake comes out clean. When fully cooked the cake should spring back when lightly touched and it should have slightly shrunk away from the sides of the tin. Leave the cake to cool in the tin for 2 – 3 minutes, then turn it out onto a wire rack or sugared paper.

Makes a 20cm (8 inch) round cake

MADEIRA CAKE

185g (6 oz/¾ cup) unsalted butter
185g (6 oz/¾ cup) caster (superfine) sugar
4 large eggs
185g (6 oz/1½ cups) self-raising flour
90 (3 oz/¾ cup) plain (all-purpose) flour
1 teaspoon lemon juice
EQUIPMENT
20cm (8 inch) round cake tin (pan)
non-stick baking spray, non-stick paper or
teflon-coated baking sheet

Preheat the oven to 160°C (325°F/Gas 3). Spray the tin (pan) with non-stick baking spray or grease and line it with non-stick paper or teflon-coated baking sheet.

Cream the butter and sugar until light and fluffy. Gradually mix in the eggs, adding a spoonful of the flour. Sift the flours together thoroughly and fold them into the mixture. Fold in the lemon juice and turn the mixture into the prepared tin.

Bake for about 1 hour 10 minutes, or until a skewer inserted in the centre of the cake comes out clean. Leave the cake to cool in the tin for 2 – 3 minutes, then turn it out onto a wire rack or sugared paper.

Makes a 20cm (8 inch) round cake

QUICK MADEIRA CAKE

500g (1 lb/4 cups) plain (all-purpose) flour
2 teaspoons baking powder
440g (14 oz/2 cups) caster (superfine) sugar
440g (14 oz/2 cups) soft margarine
7 eggs
3½ tablespoons milk
EQUIPMENT
20cm (8 inch) square or 23cm (9 inch) round cake tin (pan)
non-stick baking spray, non-stick paper or teflon-coated baking sheet

Preheat the oven to 160°C (325°F/Gas 3). Spray the tin (pan) with non-stick baking spray or grease and line it with non-stick paper or teflon-coated baking sheet. Sift the flour and baking powder into a bowl. Add the sugar, margarine, eggs and milk, and mix together. Beat for 1 minute if using an electric mixer or for 2 – 3 minutes by hand.

Turn the mixture into the prepared tin and bake for 1¾ – 2 hours, or until a skewer inserted into the centre of the cake comes out clean.

Makes a 20cm (8 inch) square or 23cm (9 inch) round cake

Sponge cakes are light and quick to make. Three classic recipes are shown here.
Top to bottom: *Sponge Cake, Swiss (Jelly) Roll and Madeira Cake*

GINGERBREAD

500g (1 lb/4 cups) plain (all-purpose) flour
1 rounded teaspoon bicarbonate of soda (baking soda)
2 teaspoons ground ginger
185g (6 oz/¾ cup) butter or margarine
315g (10 oz/2 cups) dark soft brown sugar
186g (6 oz/½ cup) golden syrup (light corn syrup)
2 eggs, lightly beaten
EQUIPMENT
baking sheets
non-stick baking spray, non-stick paper or
teflon-coated baking sheet

Preheat the oven to 190°C (375°F/Gas 5). Spray the baking sheets with non-stick baking spray or grease and line them with non-stick paper or teflon-coated baking sheet. Sift the flour, bicarbonate of soda and ground ginger together. Rub in the butter or margarine until the mixture resembles fine breadcrumbs, then add the sugar and mix well.

Warm the syrup sufficiently to make it flow easily and stir it into the rubbed-in mixture with the egg to make a pliable dough. Knead the dough until smooth, then roll it out thinly on a floured worksurface. Cut out the required shapes and place them carefully on the baking sheets. Bake for 8 – 10 minutes, until evenly browned.

Makes 1.25kg (2½ lb), about 40.5 x 30cm
(17 x 12 inch) rolled out

BOILED FRUIT CAKE

250g (8 oz/2 cups) butter or margarine
185g (6 oz/1 cup) soft brown sugar
4 tablespoons black treacle or molasses
4 teaspoons ground mixed spice (apple-pie spice)
1 teaspoon almond essence (extract)
1 teaspoon vanilla essence (extract)
1.5kg (3 lb/9 cups) mixed dried fruit
4 tablespoons brandy, sherry or orange juice
4 eggs
315 g (10 oz/2½ cups) plain (all-purpose) or
self-raising (self-rising) flour
EQUIPMENT
23cm (9 inch) round cake tin (pan)
non-stick paper or brown paper

Mix the butter or margarine, sugar, treacle or molasses, ground mixed spice, almond and vanilla essences, dried fruit and brandy, sherry or orange juice in a large saucepan and heat gently for 5 minutes until the sugar has dissolved and the ingredients are well combined. Allow the mixture to cool, then add the eggs and stir in the flour.

Turn the mixture into the prepared tin (pan) and bake for 4 hours, until a skewer inserted into the centre of the cake comes out clean. Leave the cake to cool before turning it out of the tin.

Makes a 23cm (9 inch) round cake

LIGHT FRUIT CAKE

250g (8 oz/1½ cups) mixed dried fruit
60ml (2 fl oz/¼ cup) sherry or orange juice
250g (8 oz/1 cup) butter or margarine
250g (8 oz/1¼ cups) caster (superfine) sugar
4 eggs, lightly beaten
250g (8 oz/2 cups) plain (all-purpose) flour
EQUIPMENT
20cm (8 inch) round cake tin (pan)
non-stick paper or brown paper

Soak the mixed dried fruit in the sherry or orange juice overnight to plump out the fruit. Preheat the oven to 160°C (325°F/Gas 3). Line the tin (pan) with non-stick or brown paper.

Cream the butter and sugar until light and fluffy. Gradually add the eggs. Stir in the soaked fruit, then gently fold in the flour. Turn the mixture into the tin, smooth the top, making a slight dip in the centre and bake for 1½ hours. Leave the cake to cool before turning it out of the tin.

Makes a 20cm (8 inch) round cake

RICH FRUIT CAKE

250g (8 oz/1½ cups) sultanas (golden raisins)
250g (8 oz/1⅓ cups) currants
250g (8 oz/1½ cups) raisins
125g (4 oz/⅔ cup) glacé (candied) cherries, halved
60g (2 oz/⅓ cup) blanched almonds, chopped
125ml (4 fl oz/½ cup) brandy, sherry or orange juice
250g (8 oz/2 cups) plain (all-purpose) flour
60g (2 oz/½ cup) self-raising (self-rising) flour
1 teaspoon each of ground mixed spice (apple-pie
spice) and ground cinnamon
¼ teaspoon grated nutmeg
pinch of salt
60g (2 oz/½ cup) ground almonds
250g (8 oz/1 cup) butter
250g (8 oz/1½ cups) dark soft brown sugar
4 eggs, lightly beaten
EQUIPMENT
20cm (8 inch) round cake tin (pan)
non-stick paper or brown paper

🌿 Soak the dried fruit, cherries and chopped almonds overnight in the brandy, sherry or orange juice.

🌿 Preheat the oven 140°C (275°F/Gas 1). Line the tin (pan) with non-stick or brown paper. Sift both flours, the spices and ground almonds together. Cream the butter and sugar together until light and soft, then gradually add the eggs. Stir in the flour and fruit, adding a little at a time of first one, then the other. Do not beat.

🌿 Turn the mixture into the prepared tin and bake for 3½ – 4 hours, until a skewer inserted into the centre of the cake comes out clean. Leave the cake to cool in the tin.

Fruit cakes are usually favoured for important celebrations and the alternative varieties are illustrated here.
Top to bottom: *Boiled Fruit Cake, Light Fruit Cake and traditional Rich Fruit Cake.*

COATINGS AND ICINGS

MARZIPAN

This quick-drying marzipan or almond paste is not oily and it will remain pliable for 3 – 4 weeks with correct storage. It is best to make the almond paste the day before it is required.

500g (1 lb/2 cups) sugar
155ml (5 fl oz/⅔ cup) plus 4 tablespoons water
large pinch of cream of tartar
375g (12 oz/3½ cups) ground almonds
2 egg whites
about 450g (1 lb/3 cups) icing (confectioners') sugar, sifted
almond essence (extract), optional
EQUIPMENT
sugar thermometer
marble slab or heavy-duty chopping board
metal spatula

🍃 Warm the sugar and water in a large saucepan over very gentle heat. Stir with a metal spoon to dissolve the sugar. Do not boil until every grain of sugar has dissolved. Add the cream of tartar, then bring the syrup to the boil. Boil rapidly, without stirring, until the syrup reaches 118°C (245°F), the soft ball stage.

🍃 Do not overboil as this will make the almond paste difficult to handle. To test the syrup, drop a teaspoonful of it into a cup of cold water – it should form a soft ball when removed and rubbed between the fingers. Stop the syrup cooking by placing the base of the saucepan in cold water, then immediately stir in the ground almonds and egg whites. Return the pan to low heat and stir until the mixture thickens slightly.

🍃 Turn the paste out onto a marble slab or heavy-duty chopping board and work it with a metal spatula, scraping it from the edges to the middle in a folding motion, until it cools and thickens. When the paste is cool, knead it by hand until it is smooth, working in the icing (confectioners') sugar. It will take up to half its weight in icing sugar. For extra flavour, add a few drops of almond essence. Store the paste in an airtight jar or a thick polythene bag until ready to use.

Makes 1kg (2lb)

BOILED SUGARPASTE

This recipe makes an elastic sugarpaste that is easy to handle: make it at least a day prior to use.

30g (1 oz/2 tablespoons) powdered gelatine
315ml (10 fl oz/1¼ cups) water
500g (1 lb/2 cups) sugar
125g (4 oz/⅓ cup) liquid glucose (clear corn syrup)
1 tablespoon glycerine (glycerol)
1 teaspoon cream of tartar
125g (4 oz/½ cup) white vegetable fat (shortening)
1.5kg (3 lb/9 cups) icing (confectioners') sugar, sifted
EQUIPMENT
sugar thermometer
metal spatula

🍃 Sprinkle the gelatine over half the water in a small heatproof bowl. Leave to soften for 2 – 3 minutes, until spongy. Stand the bowl over a saucepan of hot (not boiling) water and stir the gelatine until it has dissolved completely.

🍃 Meanwhile, place the sugar, glucose (clear corn syrup), glycerine (glycerol), cream of tartar and the remaining water in a wide, heavy-based saucepan over medium heat and stir until every grain of sugar has dissolved. Bring to the boil, making sure no sugar crystals adhere to the side of the saucepan. Boil over high heat until the temperature reaches 118°C (245°F), the soft ball stage.

🍃 Remove the pan from the heat immediately and place it in a bowl of cold water to stop the cooking process. Cool for 3 – 4 minutes, then stir in the fat (shortening) and the dissolved gelatine.

🍃 Mix in the icing (confectioners') sugar a cupful at a time to make a soft paste, then knead in the remaining sugar until smooth and pliable. Leave in an airtight container for 24 hours before use. If necessary, knead in extra icing sugar to obtain a dry, non-sticky consistency.

Makes about 2.5kg (5 lb)

UNCOOKED SUGARPASTE

This recipe is simple to make; however, it does not have the fine texture or elasticity of boiled sugarpaste.

2 teaspoons liquid glucose (clear corn syrup)
1 egg white
1kg (2 lb/6 cups) icing (confectioners') sugar
½ teaspoon glycerine (glycerol)
juice of ½ lemon

🍂 Warm the glucose over hot water to make it runny. Beat the egg white and add 375g (12 oz/2¼ cups) of the icing (confectioners') sugar. Beat well until the mixture begins to stiffen. Add the lemon juice and beat again. Mix in another 250g (8 oz/1½ cups) of the sugar and beat thoroughly. Add the glycerine (glycerol) and glucose (clear corn syrup) and continue beating in more icing sugar until the mixture thickens.

🍂 Once the paste is stiff, turn it out onto a worksurface dusted with icing (confectioners') sugar and knead it until it loses all signs of stickiness. The paste can be used immediately but is best placed in an airtight container and left overnight.

Makes about 1kg (2 lb)

AMERICAN BUTTERCREAM

This freezes well. It may also be made with half butter and half white vegetable fat (shortening).

125g (4 oz/½ cup) white vegetable fat (shortening)
1 teaspoon vanilla or butter essence (extract)
pinch of salt
500g (1 lb/3 cups) icing (confectioners') sugar
3 tablespoons milk

🍂 Beat the fat until it is soft, then add the vanilla or butter essence and salt. Beat in the icing (confectioners') sugar a little at a time, scraping down the sides of the bowl regularly. Add the milk and beat at high speed, until the buttercream is light and fluffy. Keep well covered in the refrigerator when not in use.

Makes about 625g (1¼ lb/3½ cups)

ROYAL ICING

5 teaspoons pure powdered albumen
90ml (3 fl oz) water
500g (1 lb/3 cups) icing (confectioners') sugar, sifted
1 teaspoon glycerine (glycerol), see method

🍂 Stir the albumen into the water and leave for 30 minutes, until it has dissolved completely. Strain the albumen into a bowl and add half the icing (confectioners') sugar. Beat the mixture on the slowest speed if using an electric mixer, or for 100 strokes by hand, until it is smooth. Add the icing to the remaining sugar and continue beating for about 10 minutes on low speed. The icing is the right consistency when it has a satin-like appearance and it stands in soft peaks.

🍂 Add the glycerine (glycerol) if the icing is to be used for covering a cake. This prevents the icing from setting too hard. Glycerine is not added to icing which is used for piping or run-outs.

Makes about 500g (1 lb)

ROYAL ICING MADE WITH FRESH EGG WHITE

🍂 Royal icing can also be made with fresh egg white. Allow 375g (12 oz/2 cups) icing (confectioners') sugar to 1 egg white. Break up the egg white with a palette knife and add the icing sugar a dessertspoonful at a time. Beat it thoroughly by hand between additions of sugar. A squeeze of lemon juice will help to give the icing a whiter appearance.

GUM ARABIC GLUE

3 teaspoons water
1 teaspoon gum arabic

🍂 Measure the water into a small screw-top jar and add the gum arabic. Shake well until the gum arabic has dissolved. Keep the mixture in the refrigerator when not in use.

PASTILLAGE

There are many different recipes for pastillage, which is also called gum paste, mexican paste, flower paste and petal paste. For convenience I use a purchased mix which is made up by adding water. There are some occasions when the paste dries too quickly, so to overcome this I mix the made-up pastillage with sugarpaste. Most pastillage becomes more elastic and easier to use if it is made up the day before it is required.

GUM PASTE (1)

250g (8 oz/1½ cups) icing (confectioners') sugar, sifted
3 teaspoons gum tragacanth or CMC
1 teaspoon liquid glucose (clear corn syrup)
5 – 6 teaspoons cold water

🦃 Sift the icing (confectioners') sugar and gum tragacanth or CMC together. Make a depression in the middle of the sugar and add the liquid glucose (clear corn syrup). Add the water and mix well. Knead well until smooth and pliable. Wrap tightly in polythene and place in an airtight container, then leave for 24 hours.

GUM PASTE (2)

500g (1 lb/3 cups) icing (confectioners') sugar , sifted
1 large egg white
3 teaspoons gum tragacanth or CMC
2 teaspoons liquid glucose (clear corn syrup)
2 teaspoons powdered gelatine
5 teaspoons cold water
2 teaspoons white vegetable fat (shortening)
EQUIPMENT
electric mixer

🦃 Warm the sugar and gum tragacanth or CMC in a large bowl over a saucepan of hot water. Cover the bowl, so that the sugar does not form a crust. Sprinkle the gelatine over the water and set aside for 30 minutes. Melt the liquid glucose (clear corn syrup), fat (shortening) and gelatine over very low heat.

🦃 Once the sugar is warm, stir it on slow speed. Add the liquid mixture and the egg white. Turn the machine to maximum speed and beat the paste for about 15 minutes. The longer and harder it is beaten, the whiter the paste will become.

GUM PASTE (3)

75g (2½ oz) egg white
500g (1 lb/3 cups) icing (confectioners') sugar, sifted
3 tablespoons Tylose, gum tragacanth or CMC
1 tablespoon white vegetable fat (shortening)
cornflour (cornstarch), see method

🦃 Make up royal icing with the egg white and sugar, see page 9. Then add the Tylose, gum tragacanth or CMC and mix well. The mixture will immediately start to thicken.

🦃 Turn the paste out onto a board dusted with icing (confectioners') sugar and knead in the fat (shortening). Wrap the paste well and place in an airtight container, then leave it for at least 24 hours. Knead the paste again. If the paste seems sticky, add a little icing sugar or cornflour (cornstarch).

EDIBLE GUM

Gum tragacanth is an edible plant gum which has been put to various culinary uses for centuries. It has been used for many years to harden gum pastes. CMC stands for carboxymethyl cellulose, a man-made edible gum. Tylose is a brand name for a particular type of CMC. These gums are used to make the paste more elastic and pliable.

THICKNESS GUIDE

Use the diagram shown here to give the correct thickness for sugarpaste and pastillage.

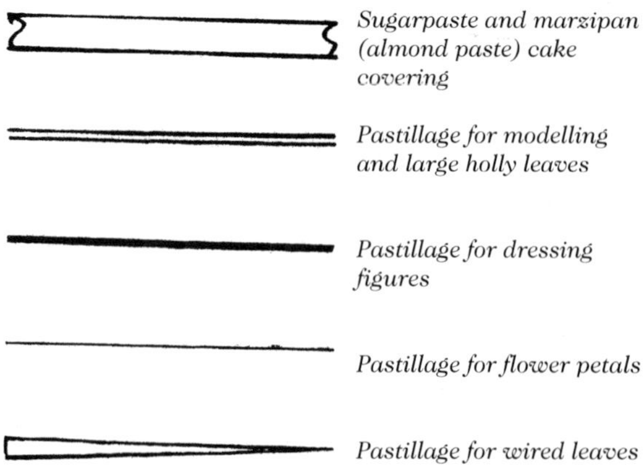

Sugarpaste and marzipan (almond paste) cake covering

Pastillage for modelling and large holly leaves

Pastillage for dressing figures

Pastillage for flower petals

Pastillage for wired leaves

BASIC TECHNIQUES

COATING CAKES WITH MARZIPAN

If the cake is to be covered with sugarpaste, then the marzipan (almond paste) is applied in the same way. Trim the top edge of the cake with a sausage of marzipan, then turn the cake over and brush it with boiled, sieved apricot jam or piping gel. Roll out enough marzipan to cover the top and sides of the cake and follow the instructions given on the right. Allow the marzipan to harden for 24 hours.

If a cake is to be royal iced, the method is as follows and the bottom of the cake is the surface to be iced.

1 Roll out a sausage of marzipan and lay it around the top edge of the cake, sticking it in place with boiled, sieved apricot jam or piping gel. Roll out the marzipan larger than the cake and brush with piping gel. Stand the cake on the paste and trim the bottom edge with a palette knife.

2 Roll out a long, rectangular strip of marzipan measuring three times the diameter of a round cake . Brush the paste with piping gel. Place the cake at one end of the strip, then roll it onto the paste. Press the marzipan gently into place with a smoother, so that the top edge is square and smooth.

COATING CAKES WITH SUGARPASTE

Sugarpaste is flexible and fairly elastic, rather like uncooked pastry, so it follows the contours of a cake very accurately, making it ideal for covering cakes of uneven or irregular shapes. In fact, it is helpful if the edges and corners over which the sugarpaste is laid are not too sharp. For this reason, if a cake is covered with marzipan (almond paste), it is best to drape the marzipan across the entire surface in one piece, rather than covering the top and sides separately.

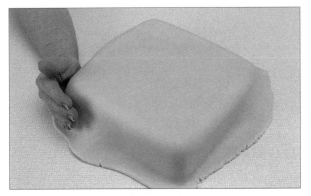

1 Sugarpaste is rolled out and draped over a cake. Always smooth the paste onto the corners first, using the palm of your hand to work it firmly onto the cake. Do not allow the paste to form pleats – if necessary, flare it outwards gently, then squeeze it back against the side of the cake.

2 Use two smoothers to smooth the paste: hold the cake steady with one while using an ironing action with the other to flatten and smooth the icing. Work on the sides, then the cake top. When the top is satisfactory, finish the sides, paying special attention to the edges and corners.

COATING CAKES WITH ROYAL ICING

The action of beating together the sugar and egg gives royal icing its biscuit-like texture by incorporating millions of tiny bubbles. Icing which is inadequately beaten will be hard and will crumble and crack when it is cut. Well-made icing can be cut easily with a sharp knife.

It is very important to ensure that the bowl in which you make royal icing is completely free of grease as any contamination prevents the mixture from becoming properly aerated. It is also advisable to beat royal icing in a metal or china bowl rather than plastic which is more difficult to wash completely clean.

If you are concerned about the dangers of salmonella from fresh eggs, the icing can be made from dried, pasteurised powdered egg white or albumen. Simply mix the albumen with water, let it dissolve properly and use it in the same way as fresh egg white. Albumen is also ideal for meringues.

Adding a few drops of lemon juice to royal icing will help to whiten it and also give it a little extra elasticity. This is an advantage when you are using fine piping tubes (tips); but it makes the icing more brittle, so do not add lemon juice to icing used for covering cakes. Allow 1 teaspoon glycerine (glycerol) to each 500 g (1 lb/3 cups) of icing (confectioners') sugar used to make icing for coating a little softer when it has dried on the cake.

A really smooth finish requires at least three separate applications of icing and each layer should dry for a day before the next is applied. Therefore, you must allow plenty of time when coating a cake with royal icing.

1 *Apply royal icing across the top of the cake with a palette knife. Spread the icing from side to side in a paddling motion until it is evenly dispersed, rotating the turntable at the same time. Pressing and working the icing with the knife blade helps to burst any air bubbles it contains.*

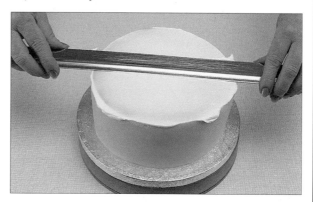

2 *Smooth the icing with a metal straight edge. Beginning at the far side of the cake, draw the blade steadily towards you. When you reach the near side, turn the blade over so that its other edge is touching the icing, and push it away from you to the far side of the cake. Do this three or four times. By turning the straight edge over, the icing only builds up on one side.*

3 *Use a scraper to smooth the icing around the cake sides. Hold it at an angle of about 45 degrees to the cake and rotate the cake through one complete turn of the turntable. The secret of a smooth finish is to rotate the turntable and the cake while holding the scraper steady.*

PIPING TECHNIQUES

It is important to check that the royal icing is of a suitable consistency. Day-old icing is best for most purposes, as the ingredients will have become thoroughly mixed on standing. Always remember to beat the icing by hand in a clean bowl using a palette knife before transferring to a piping bag. The icing should be light and fluffy, and it should hold a firm peak, sinking very slowly back when you test it with the knife blade.

A paper piping bag is far easier to use than an icing syringe. Paper bags should be made of vegetable parchment as this remains waterproof for several hours, so the bags do not split open as easily as those made of greaseproof paper.

MAKING A PIPING BAG

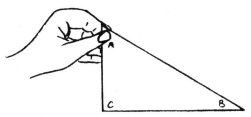

1 Cut a triangle of vegetable parchment paper and hold the shortest side closest to your wrist, point A on the diagram.

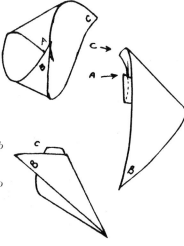

2 Take point B in the other hand, move it away from you, then up and over the back of the fingers holding point A.

3 Draw point B steadily towards you and, at the same time, slide the edge of the paper under the thumb holding point A.

4 The cone will start to take shape; continue wrapping point B around it, keeping the paper taut.

5 This makes a cone with a sharp point. Change your grip and fold the loose ends of the parchment into the bag. Tear a small flap into the fold line to lock the layers of paper together.

To pipe a straight line, touch the point of the piping tube (tip) to the surface, then, keeping constant pressure , lift the bag and let the icing flow steadily. Keep the point of the tube (tip) about 5 cm (2 inch) above the surface. Neither squeeze the bag too hard nor pull at the icing, or the strand will snap.

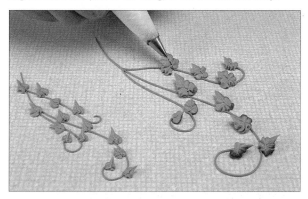

Leaves are usually piped with a special piping tube (tip). Hold the bag at a 45 degree angle and squeeze it fairly hard at first, jiggling the bag at the same time. As each leaf begins to form, relax the pressure and withdraw the bag in one motion. This action pulls the icing into a point, forming the leaf tip.

It is important to control the rate at which the icing is squeezed out of the piping tube (tip). These stars are all made with a no. 7 star piping tube (tip). They show the difference made by varying the pressure. The bag is held in a vertical position when piping stars.

Shells vary in size according to the pressure applied. Hold the bag at an angle of 45 degrees to the surface and push out the icing to form the fattest part of the shell, then release the pressure on the bag, and pull the piping tube (tip) straight back. Place the piping tube (tip) directly behind the tail of the shell just piped and pipe another which covers its tail.

Scrolls are piped with a star piping tube (tip). To taper them, begin by squeezing the bag steadily while moving the point of the piping tube (tip) slowly. As you near the end of each scroll relax the pressure and increase the rate at which you move the bag. Practise piping scrolls in each direction so that you form 'C' and 'S' shapes.

FLOODING

This type of painting with icing is described as flooding, run-out work or run-in work. It is a very effective technique which can be employed to create detailed pictures in bold colours. Run-out or run-in designs are often piped onto waxed paper or on a teflon-coated non-stick mat, in which case an outline is piped first and then it is filled with thinned royal icing. Flooding is usually carried out directly on the iced surface without piping an outline.

Whichever method you use, the royal icing should have the same consistency. Make up fresh icing to normal piping consistency, then add water, a few drops at a time, and stir gently – do not beat the icing. To determine whether the icing is sufficiently runny, swirl it

with a knife and count steadily to ten. After 10 seconds, the swirls should have subsided and the surface of the icing should be smooth again.

Piped outlines form a boundary to prevent the icing overflowing the edge of a design. Theoutlines should be piped using icing of a normal consistency and a no. 0 or no. 1 piping tube (tip). Flooding icing will form a skin very quickly, so have a brush ready to push it right up to the piped outlines. Also, use the brush to burst any air bubbles that may appear in the icing.

When creating a complicated design, work in different sections of the picture at the same time. It is important to avoid having two wet areas side by side, as one will bleed into the other. Shine an anglepoise lamp onto the design so that the icing dries while you work. The warmth will also help the icing to dry with a good shine.

These trees and parcels are piped onto a transparent teflon-coated mat with the design underneath. Pipe the outline first to prevent the icing flowing over the edge of the design edge. Then use a piping bag with a very small hole cut at the point of the bag.

With practice you can work directly onto a cake without a piped outline. Keep the piping tube (tip) point in the icing as it flows. Use a fine paintbrush to break air bubbles and to direct the icing. It only takes minutes for the icing to form a skin. Then you can fill neighbouring areas.

USING PASTILLAGE

Pastillage has many uses and most ornaments, sugar flowers and leaves are made using this versatile medium as there are many ways of enhancing its appearance with colours and glazing.

When you are actually working with the paste, temporarily store the pieces you intend to use in a polythene bag. When it is rolled very thin, pastillage dries within minutes, so immediately cover any rolled pieces which are not in use. I use a very thick piece of clear plastic material, my 'floppy mat', for this purpose.

Keep any unused paste in good condition by wrapping it in plastic wrap, then placing it in an airtight plastic container before putting it in the refrigerator. Most mixtures can be stored in this way for several weeks but it is important to knead them occasionally so that the paste retains its elasticity and malleability.

DUSTING WITH COLOUR

Dusting powder is used to achieve subtle gradations of colour on pastillage. Apply the powders to hardened paste using a fairly large brush. Stipple the colour on, working from the outside edge into the middle of the flower or leaf. Always work on a piece of kitchen roll or tissue as it is easier to clean up when you have finished. This technique is illustrated on page 42 for colouring the flame on the Holly Cake.

CUTTING PASTILLAGE

Thin sections of pastillage can be cut very accurately with a long-bladed knife. Use a guillotine action to cut the paste. Do not drag the tip of the blade through the paste as this causes it to stretch and distort.

MAKING PASTILLAGE LEAVES

1 To create realistic pastillage leaves, mark their surface by pressing them against a special veining tool while they are still soft. Cutters and tools for this purpose are available in plastic and metal, in a wide variety of shapes and patterns.

2 Leaves look best if they are allowed to harden into twisted and bent shapes. Drape the soft leaves over crinkled foil and leave them to harden. Then dip them in confectioners' glaze.

3 Confectioners' glaze is an edible varnish used to preserve sugar models. Holly leaves and seals from the cake on page 32 are shown here both before and after they have been glazed. Small items can be dipped into the bowl of glaze, while larger ones are usually painted with glaze.

BASIC MODELLING

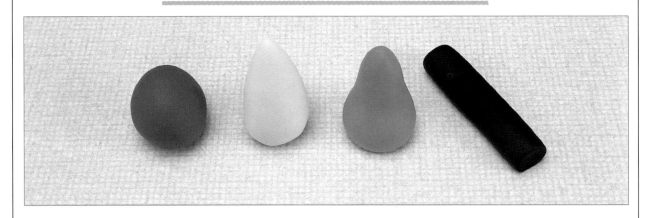

If you have never tried modelling, why not make the simple animals and objects shown on the next few pages? Almost all of them are derived from four basic shapes – the ball, the cone, the pear and the sausage.

These four basic shapes are modelled by hand. Use the palms of the hands to roll ball shapes and the edges and sides of the hands to form the pear and cone. Roll the sausage shape on the worksurface to obtain an even result.

Although a set of modelling tools makes a very useful addition to the cake decorator's workbox, most of these figures can be made using only a craft knife and a pair of fine-pointed scissors.

Figures are often made to look comical by modelling their heads much larger in proportion to their bodies than they would be in the real world, and a ratio of 3:5 seems to work well in most cases. For example, if you make a figure with a head which weighs about 30g (1 oz), the main part of the body should weigh about 50g (1¾ oz). For more realistic models, or those formed in moulds, the proportions should be as close as possible to reality.

The simple shapes shown on the following pages are all made using a paste combining sugarpaste pastillage in equal quantities.

The four basic shapes: ball, cone, pear and sausage.

THE BALL

Shaping a ball is the most fundamental technique for all modelling as the action achieves a smooth surface on all sides of the paste. Place the paste between the palms of the hands and roll it strongly in a circular motion. Having achieved the basic shape, roll the paste more gently and uniformly, raising the hands to chin level. In this position the eye can follow the working of the paste and you will be able to see if there are any irregularities in the surface of the ball.

The ball is used for the heads of many of the models shown in this book. The basic steps are always similar. Use a dogbone modelling tool to make sockets for the eyes and a cone-shaped tool to make a socket for the nose. Then pipe the features. In this illustration, the head is enclosed in a hood of blue paste. Similar finished figures may be seen on pages 19, Father Christmas, and 33, eskimos.

THE CONE

Roll a ball in the palms of the hands to ensure that the surface is smooth, then turn the upper hand so that the edge of the palm is resting on one side of the ball. Slide the upper hand diagonally several times over the ball and it will form a cone. To elongate the cone, position it so that its point is between the heels of both hands and gently rub them together. This will cause the point of the cone to extend and become thinner.

MAKING HANDS

One of the most widely used applications of the cone is for making hands. Take a small cone of paste and flatten the broad end. Use fine-pointed scissors to snip a V-shaped section out of one side to create a thumb. Make three small cuts to form the fingers. Do not make these cuts too deep, as the base of the fingers should extend only a little way beyond the tip of the thumb. Curve the fingers so that the hand appears relaxed.

THE PEAR

The pear shape is formed from a cone. Place the cone between the heels of the hands and adjust the position of the upper hand so that it is slightly higher on the cone, then rub it against the palm of the lower hand. This will cause the cone to bulge slightly. This basic pear shape can be elongated at either end using the same basic action to form all sorts of animal bodies.

THE SAUSAGE

As usual, start by modelling a ball to give the paste a smooth surface. If you try to roll the paste into a sausage between your hands, it becomes more of a cigar shape as it tends to become thicker in the middle and tapered at the ends. Roll the paste on the worksurface, making sure that you use the palm or heel of the hand rather than the fingers which make lumpy sausages as the paste is pressed into the spaces between the fingers.

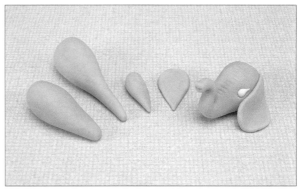

A cone, when elongated, twisted into shape and finished with a modelling tool, becomes the head of a trumpeting elephant! The two-coloured ears are made by sticking thinly rolled grey and pink pastillage together. Stick them into position with gum arabic glue.

Two pear shapes form a polar bear. The larger pear forms the bear's body and the smaller one makes the head. The mouth is made by snipping the paste with scissors. Press tiny balls of paste into the soft head with a small ball tool to make ears. Model four small sausage shapes for legs. Use black icing to highlight the bear's features.

A tiny sausage of black paste assumes the shape of a seal when one end is split, then squeezed with a ridged modelling tool. Cut the front flippers by snipping the paste away from the body with scissors, bending the flippers forward. Indent the neck slightly and shape the nose to a blunt point.

TOYS

All sorts of figures and toys can be made in a variety of sizes using the basic shapes.

BUS

Shape a rectangular block of red paste using a blunt knife and cut out the door at the back. Use tiny pieces of white or black paste for the windows, wheels, lights and radiator, and stick them in place with gum arabic glue, see page 9. Use a food colour pen to paint the markings on the windows and radiators.

YACHT

Roll out white pastillage and cut out two triangles for the sails, then leave them to dry for at least a few hours. Model a sausage and roll it to a point at each end, then flatten it along one side. Pinch out the opposite side to form the keel. Then stick the sails into the hull while the paste is still soft.

TRAIN

A toy train does not have to look like the real thing. Roll a sausage for the engine and a ball for the cab. Indent one side of the cab with a large ball tool to make it hollow, then cut the side shapes with a pair of fine-pointed scissors. Make a very small cone for the funnel and mark the wheels with a modelling knife. Pipe a red dot on the front of the engine and a pair of eyes on the front of the cab.

DOLL

This little rag doll is less than 10cm (4 inch) tall. Shape a cone for the body and split the pointed end into two using a sharp craft knife. Blue pastillage has been used for the clothing: roll the pastillage very thin and frill it, see page 20, before wrapping it around the body. Use a rectangle of blue paste for the bodice and add white strips of paste for the belt. Dress all the limbs before joining the arms and head to the torso. Use yellow paste for the hair.

EGG PEOPLE AND CHRISTMAS TREES

These ornaments are completely edible and simple to make. The trees are piped over wafer ice-cream cornets and the figures are all made on sugar-coated chocolate eggs. The garments on the figures are made from thinly rolled pastillage and they are attached with Gum Arabic Glue, see page 9. Larger pieces, such as the heads and the arms, can also be secured with gum arabic glue or with suitably coloured royal icing for extra strength. Some parts of the models have to be dry before the finishing touches can be added, so make them in stages over two or more days.

750g (1½ lb) Sugarpaste, see page 8
500g (1 lb) Pastillage, see page 10
red, blue, black, skintone, green, Cornish cream, dark brown and peach paste colours
4 sugar-coated chocolate eggs
250 g (8 oz/ 1 cup) Royal Icing, see page 9
Gum Arabic Glue, see page 9
3 ice-cream wafer cones
red, silver and gold coloured dragees (nonpareils)
rice paper

EQUIPMENT
fluted garrett frill cutter
baby face mould
set of modelling tools
10 and 7.5cm (4 and 3 inch) round cutters
nos. 51 and 52 leaf piping tubes (tips), no. 5
star piping tube (tip) and nos. 0, 1 and 2
writing tubes (tips)
piping bags
scriber
paintbrushes
small teardrop (rose petal) cutter
small blossom plunger cutter
jasmine cutter
cocktail stick (toothpick)
no. 30 mini single scallop crimper
small carnation or fluted cutter

Mix 440g (14 oz) each of sugarpaste and pastillage together and knead until thoroughly combined. Leave 250g (8 oz) paste white. Colour 90g (3 oz) paste black, 185g (6 oz) skintone, 155g (5 oz) blue and 185g (6 oz) red. Before starting any of the models, cut a circle or plaque of sugarpaste for each egg. Attach the eggs to the plaques with royal icing, placing the pointed ends up. Leave to set for 24 hours.

CHOIR BOY OR GIRL

Make the face and head in one piece by pressing a 60g (2 oz) ball of skintone paste into the lightly greased baby face mould. Model the back of the head by hand, then remove from the mould. Define the mouth, if necessary, with a small ball tool. Dry overnight.

Paint the features with food colour using a fine paint-brush. Then pipe the hair using a no.1 piping tube (tip) with brown royal icing. Swirl the icing with a dampened brush to fill in any gaps. Leave to dry for about 1 hour.

Use a small rose petal cutter to cut out shoes from black paste and stick them to the plaque. Indent the shoes with the rose petal cutter to form the toe caps and mark holes for laces using the cone modelling tool. Cut a small rectangle of black paste for the book and support it in the open shape. Dry on wax paper.

Roll out blue paste to make the surplice and cut a 10cm (4 inch) circle. Paint the top of the egg with gum arabic glue and drape the paste centrally over it. Use a garrett frill cutter to cut out a scalloped circle of paste and use the small blossom plunger cutter to mark the scalloped edge to create a lacy effect, then drape this over the

surplice, sticking it in place with gum arabic glue. Make two pleats to give the impression that the figure has outstretched arms beneath the cape.

Cut a small star with the jasmine cutter and stick this to the top of the egg. Then stick the head in position with royal icing, hiding any excess icing by lifting the points of the star to form a collar. Make the pages of the book by rolling out a very thin rectangle of white paste and sticking it into the black cover. Support the book in front of the choir boy on a foam pad, then use a no. 2 piping tube (tip) and skintone royal icing to pipe the hands. Once dry, the icing will hold the book in place.

ANGEL

Make a head as for the choir boy but do not mark the open mouth. Pipe the hair using a no. 0 piping tube (tip) and yellow royal icing, squeezing it onto the head from a distance of 1cm (½ inch) so that it drops in loops and curls. While the icing is still wet, cut a halo from a circle of rice paper and stick it to the back of the head.

Cut a 12cm (4.5 inch) circle of paste for the dress and frill it with a cocktail stick (toothpick), see below. Use a no.30 mini single scallop crimper to decorate the edge above the frill, then drape the dress over the egg, securing it with gum arabic glue.

Make the arms and sleeves in one piece from a sausage of white paste measuring about 12cm (4½ inch) long. Use a cone modelling tool to open the cuffs, then frill the

MAKING A FRILL Frilling is a basic decorating skill which is much easier than it looks. Use a fluted cutter to stamp out the circle. Place a cocktail stick (toothpick) on the edge of the paste, then, while pressing the stick with a finger, roll it around the perimeter. This action stretches small areas of the paste, causing it to pucker behind the cocktail stick and so creating the frill.

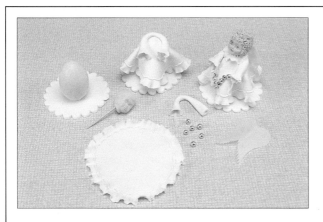

Pipe a strand of royal icing between the two hands using a no. 2 piping tube (tip) and stick gold and silver dragees onto it while the icing is still wet. For the finishing touch, add a pair of rice-paper wings.

FATHER CHRISTMAS

Start with the head, see page 16, as this needs to dry before putting the hat on. Take a 60g (2 oz) ball of skin-tone paste and indent two impressions for eyes. Use the pointed cone tool to make a hole just below the eyes for the nose. To make the nose, roll a tiny amount of paste into a cone. Use gum arabic glue to stick it in place. Allow the head to dry.

To make the boots, roll two pea-sized balls of black paste into cones. Place the point of each cone against the side of the egg and stick them in place. For the hands, take a ball of black paste about the size of a hazelnut and shape it so that it tapers to a point at each end. Use the blade of the modelling tool to mark a zig-zag pattern down the middle, then bend the pointed ends into a 'U' shape – almost like a pair of horns.

continued overleaf

edge of the paste with a cocktail stick (toothpick). Mould the hands, see page 17 and set them into the sleeves with gum arabic glue, then drape the arms around the top of the egg, securing with gum arabic glue.

Cut out a small scalloped circle using the carnation cutter and frill the edges. Glue this to the top of the egg and pipe some royal icing on it, then attach the head. Disguise the join by lifting the edge of the frill.

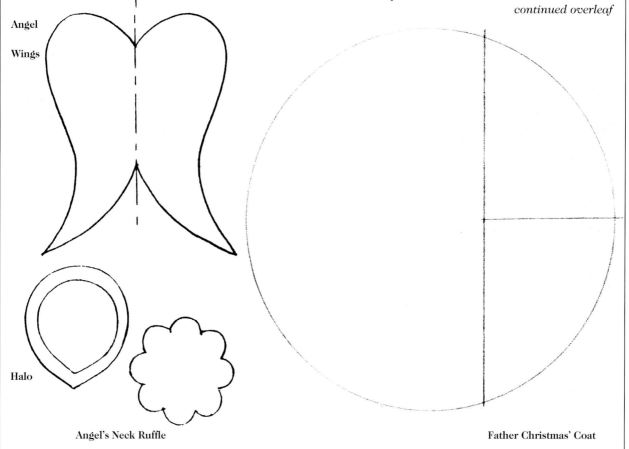

Angel

Wings

Halo

Angel's Neck Ruffle

Father Christmas' Coat

To make the coat, roll out the red paste. Cut out a 10cm (4 inch) and a 7.5cm (3 inch) circle. Then cut the larger circle as shown in the diagram, see page 21, to form the two sleeves and the coat. Paint some gum arabic glue along the edge of the larger section and drape this around the egg, overlapping the gummed edges at the front. To make the sleeves, roll the remaining sections into two cones and stick them into position with the pointed ends meeting on top of the egg. Trim the edges of the coat by using a no. 5 star piping tube (tip) to pipe a line of stiff royal icing. Stick the hands in position with the pointed ends inside each sleeve

Cut the smaller circle of red paste in half and roll one piece into a cone to make a hat. Then stick it onto the back of the head. Pipe some royal icing on the top of the egg to attach the head. Fill the eye sockets with white royal icing and leave to dry, then paint the eyeballs with black colour. Pipe the beard and moustache in white royal icing using a no. 5 star piping tube (tip).

SNOWMAN

Roll 60g (2 oz) white paste into a ball to form the head. Make two eye sockets and a hole for the nose. Use a U-shaped tool to mark the mouth. Colour a tiny amount of white paste bright orange and roll it into a carrot shape to make the nose. Attach it with gum arabic glue. Leave the head to dry.

Make the arms by rolling a sausage of paste, then cut it in half lengthways. Roll each piece to form an elongated cone and stick them to the egg with the pointed ends meeting on the top. Attach the head to the egg with royal icing. Fill the eye sockets with white royal icing and leave to dry.

To make the hat, roll a pea-sized ball of black paste and mark the centre using the blade modelling tool. Roll out

a circle of black paste and stick the ball of paste on top. Stick this hat to the head with gum arabic glue

The scarf is made from separate strands of blue, red and white paste which are twisted together to form a spiral. Flatten the spiral with a mini rolling pin, then roll it out so that the paste is quite thin. Trim the edges and cut the fringe with a sharp knife.

Finish by piping three or four buttons down the snowman's front using a no. 1 writing tube (tip) with black royal icing and pipe two black dots for the eyes .

CHRISTMAS TREES

Cut a circle of green pastillage the same size as the base of the ice-cream wafer cone. Attach the paste to the cone with green royal icing.

Model the tree trunk with brown pastillage and roughen it with a scriber so that it looks like bark. Then trim it to about 2.5cm (1 inch) long and attach it to the pastillage on the base of the cone with a little royal icing. Leave to dry overnight.

Using a no. 52 leaf piping tube (tip) and starting at the base of the cone, pipe a row of leaves. The second and subsequent rows of leaves are arranged so that the tips of the upper leaves fall between the tips of those in the row below. Two-thirds of the way up the cone, change to a smaller no. 51 leaf piping tube (tip) to complete the tree. Leave to dry.

Once the leaves are dry, the trees can by decorated with coloured dragees or dusted with icing (confectioners') sugar.

CAKE DESIGNS

Making and decorating a cake is an essential preparation for the festive season. Wherever I am, the traditional images conjured up at Christmas time are broadly similar - peace, goodwill, comfort and relaxation. Few aspects combine these ideas better than Christmas cake, freshly baked, still hot from the oven and imparting a spicy, aromatic warmth. So, when the stores are noisy and crowded, there is nothing I like better than to settle down quietly at home to decorate my family's Christmas cake. I hope to share some of this pleasure with you in the designs which follow. Happy Christmas!

EQUIPMENT

Clockwise from bottom left:
large holly cutter; rolling pin; modelling sticks; bought holly berries; large scallop crimper; small crimping tools; piping bags; piping tubes (tips); scraper; straight edge; scriber; round cutters; calyx cutter; set of poinsettia cutters; holly leaf cutters and all-in-one flower cutter; gold and silver dragees (nonpareils); smoother; paintbrushes; cranked palette knife; semi-transparent, non-stick, floppy mat; on the mat: straight frill cutter, circular garrett frill cutter and a set of modelling tools; leaf veiners.

SANTA CAKE

A royal-iced cake with shell piping and a Santa Claus cut from coloured sugarpaste makes this striking design. A bow of wide, floppy velvet ribbon adds a touch of luxury.

20cm (8 inch) round fruit cake, see page 7
875g (1¾ lb) Marzipan (almond paste), see page 8
500g (1 lb/2 cups) Royal Icing, see page 9
375g (12 oz) Sugarpaste or Marzipan (almond paste), see pages 8 and 9
red, black and skintone paste food colours
EQUIPMENT
28cm (11 inch) round cake board
no. 6 shell piping tube (tip)
large piping bags
set of 1 – 7cm (½ – 3 inch) round cutters
set of 4.5 – 6cm (1½ – 2½ inch) scalloped round cutters
1.5 metres (1¾ yd) red velvet ribbon

Cover the cake and board with marzipan (almond paste) and three layers of white royal icing. Leave to dry. Using the no. 6 shell piping tube (tip) and large piping bag filled with stiff royal icing, pipe a shell border around the top and bottom edges of the cake. Then leave to dry.

Santa Claus can be cut out of almond paste or sugarpaste. Colour 30g (1 oz) black, 60g (2 oz) skintone, 155g (5 oz) red and leave the remaining 125g (4 oz) white. Start by rolling out the red paste for the body. Cut a 7.5cm (3 inch) circle, then remove a 'V' shape section from the lower edge. Dampen the back of the circle with a little water and place it in the centre of the cake. Use the template on page 47 as a guide. Cut the arms and the hat and place them in the 10.00 and 2.00 o'clock positions.

Cut the cap from a 5cm (2 inch) circle of red paste and cut out a piece so that it fits against the top of the head. Set the cap aside until the face has been positioned. Roll out some black paste and cut a strip measuring 5mm (¼ inch) wide and 7.5cm (3 inch) long. Dampen this and place it in position to form the belt. Cut a small square to form the buckle.

To make the boots, cut a 2.5cm (1 inch) circle of black paste. Cut it in half and remove a small 'V' shape to fashion the sole and heel of each boot. Dampen the backs of the boots and position them about 5mm (¼ inch) below the body and about 1cm (½ inch) apart.

For the face, roll two very small balls of skintone paste to form the cheeks and place these on the cake about 2cm (¾ inch) above the body. Now roll out the rest of the skintone paste, cut out a 5cm (2 inch) circle and smooth it over the cheeks. The nose and mouth are just small balls of skintone and red paste, squashed slightly as they are stuck in place. Indent the mouth with the end of a paintbrush. Add two tiny balls of black paste for the eyes and tiny cigar-shaped rolls of white paste for the eyebrows.

Cut two 2cm (¾ inch) circles to form the hands. Follow the template to make the hands and stick them in place. Then build up the beard from white sugarpaste, cut with fluted cutters. Dampen the first, larger, layer of beard and place it over the lower portion of the face, then stick the smaller beard shape on top. Make the moustache from two semi-circles of paste.

Cut out 15 tiny circles and mark each with a star pattern, then use to trim the cap, coat and boots. Finally, cut another scalloped circle and use a small round cutter to cut out four sections to trim the cuffs and boots. Tie a bow of velvet ribbon around the cake.

YULE LOG

A yule log is made from a Swiss (jelly) roll and coated with chocolate buttercream. For extra effect, this one is decorated with meringue mushrooms and trailing ivy.

1 egg white
60g (2 oz/¼ cup) caster (superfine) sugar
30 x 20cm (12 x 8 inch) Swiss (Jelly) Roll, see page 4
315g (10 oz/1½ cups) American Buttercream, see page 9
1 tablespoon cocoa powder (unsweetened cocoa powder) or 2 tablespoons drinking chocolate powder plus extra for decorating
3 tablespoons chocolate liqueur or rum (optional)
brown and green paste food colours
60g (2 oz) Marzipan (almond paste), see page 8
icing (confectioners') sugar for decorating

EQUIPMENT
non-stick baking sheet
large fabric piping bag
large plain savoy piping tube (tip)
23 x 10cm (9 x 4 inch) log card
set of 3 ivy leaf cutters

Preheat the oven to 110°C(225°F/Gas ¼.) Make the meringue mushrooms by whisking the egg white until it stands in stiff peaks. Add half the sugar and whisk until the mixture is smooth and shiny. Using a large metal spoon, gently fold in the remaining sugar in two stages.

Put the meringue mixture into a large piping bag fitted with a savoy tube (tip) and pipe rounds of meringue in two sizes onto a non-stick baking sheet. Pipe small rounds for the stems and larger ones for the caps. The meringue will expand slightly as it cooks, so do not make the rounds too big. Bake the meringues for about 1 hour, until crisp and dry. Cool on a wire rack.

Reserve 60g (2 oz/generous ⅓ cup) of the buttercream. Beat the cocoa powder (unsweetened cocoa powder) or drinking chocolate powder into the rest of the buttercream and flavour it with 1 tablespoon of the chocolate liqueur or rum if liked.

Carefully unroll the cooled cake and remove the paper. Brush the cake with the remaining chocolate liqueur or rum, then spread with the chocolate buttercream and roll it up again.

Use some of the white buttercream to cover the ends of the log and spread the remainder over the log card. Use a flat-bladed knife to spread the remaining chocolate buttercream over the surface of the log and place it on the prepared card. Use brown food colour to paint the rings on the ends of the log.

Stick the caps of the mushrooms to the stalks with white buttercream and sift a little cocoa powder or drinking chocolate powder over them. Place them in position.

Colour the marzipan (almond paste) green and roll out a thin strand to form the ivy stem. Lay this over the log. Cut out about eight ivy leaves of different sizes, bend them into shape and place them against the stem. Finally, sift some icing (confectioners') sugar over the cake to give the impression of a fine dusting of snow.

VARIATIONS

The Swiss (jelly) roll may be flavoured as follows.

CHOCOLATE Add 15g (½ oz/2 tablespoons) cocoa powder (unsweetened cocoa powder) or 60g (2 oz/2 squares) grated plain (dark) chocolate to the flour.

HAZELNUT Add 30g (1 oz) ground hazelnuts to the flour.

GINGER Add 2 teaspoons ground ginger to the flour.

CITRUS Add 2 teaspoons grated orange, lemon or lime rind to the sugar.

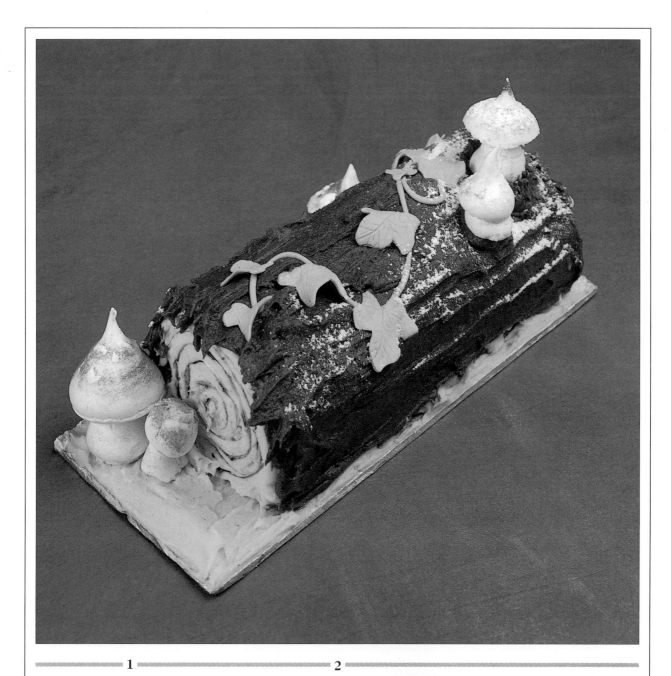

ROLLING A SWISS (JELLY) ROLL
1 Lay non-stick paper on a dampened tea-towel and sprinkle with caster (superfine) sugar. Immediately the sponge is cooked, turn it out onto the paper. Trim the cake edges and make a shallow cut 2.5cm (1 inch) in from the shorter end.
2 Lay non-stick paper over the sponge. Start rolling up the cake at the cut end, keeping the paper inside it. Use the tea-towel and sugared paper to lift the cake.

ALPINE WINTER FUN

This cake is so easy to make and it is a great favourite with the children. White buttercream and a selection of commercial cake decorations transform a bell-shaped sponge cake into a winter playground. The Dolly Varden tin (pan) is also known as a tiffin or bell tin (pan).

double quantity Sponge Cake, see page 4
20cm (8 inch) round Sponge Cake, see page 4
double quantity American Buttercream, see page 9
EQUIPMENT
large Dolly Varden tin (pan)
28 cm (11 inch) round cake board
selection of commercial decorations, for example
12 Christmas trees, 4 snowmen in different positions,
Father Christmas, reindeer and 4 snow children
10cm (4 inch) palette knife or flat-bladed knife

🍂 Preheat the oven to 160°C(325°F/Gas 3). Grease and flour the Dolly Varden tin (pan). Turn the sponge cake mixture into the tin and bake for about 1½ hours, until a skewer inserted in the centre of the cake comes out clean. Turn the cake out of the tin and leave to cool on a wire rack.

🍂 Slice the round cake into two layers and cut these into spirals, see diagram. Brush the bell-shaped cake with warmed sieved apricot jam or spread it with buttercream and jam. Make sure the buttercream is well whisked. Beginning at the base of the cake, spread a thin layer of buttercream over the surface using a palette knife. Attach a spiral of sponge cake as shown below. Then brush the spiral of cake with warmed sieved apricot jam and a thin layer of buttercream.

🍂 Place the cake in the freezer for 1 hour or in the refrigerator for 2 hours. Then apply a more generous layer of buttercream, forming it into irregular peaks. Finish the coating on the slide by warming the knife in a bowl of hot water and wiping it along the area to be smoothed. Arrange a selection of bought decorations on the icing.

Cutting the layers of sponge cake into spiral strips: start at the outer edge and work towards the middle of the cake, keeping the strip as even in width as possible.

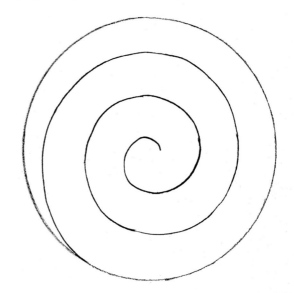

ATTACHING THE SPIRALS OF CAKE TO THE BELL-SHAPED CAKE
Slice the round cake horizontally into two 2.5cm (1 inch) thick layers. Cut both layers into spiral strips, see diagram. Then attach them around the bell-shaped cake, starting at the bottom and working up to the top.

GINGERBREAD SLEIGH

An edible gingerbread sleigh filled with sweets is an irresistible and inexpensive decoration at Christmas. Remember to keep filling it up with sweets, otherwise the sleigh itself will also be eaten by Boxing Day.

1 quantity Gingerbread, see page 6
500g (1 lb/2 cups) Royal Icing, see page 9
40 glazed holly leaves, see page 15
red and green paste food colours
selection of sweets
EQUIPMENT
scriber
large and small piping bags
no. 12 star piping tube (tip)
no. 1 piping tube (tip)

Preheat the oven to 190°C(375°F/Gas 5). Grease two baking sheets. Make the gingerbread, then roll it out to a thickness of 5mm (¼ inch) and cut out the pieces using the templates on pages 46 and 47. Turn the pattern over when cutting the sleigh's second side. Place the gingerbread on the baking sheets and bake for about 10 minutes, until evenly browned.

While the gingerbread is still hot, lay the templates over the appropriate pieces and trim them with a sharp knife. Do not wait until they are cold, as they become too crisp to cut easily. Allow the gingerbread to harden for 24 hours.

Using a scriber, mark the approximate positions for the icing garlands on the sides of the sleigh. Have something ready to support each side piece until the entire sleigh is assembled. Using a no. 12 star piping tube (tip), pipe a line of icing along one upper edge of the base and press one of the side pieces onto it. Next add the back panel: pipe some icing down one edge and along the bottom, then press it against the side panel and the base. Add the front panel in the same way and, lastly, add the second side. Pipe shells along each of the joins, both inside and out, to reinforce and embellish them.

When the sleigh has set, pipe the icing garlands on the marked side panels. The top edges are decorated with a heavier piped pattern, so exert a little more pressure on the piping bag. While the icing is still soft, stick the holly leaves in position. Let the icing dry before using a no. 1 piping tube (tip) and red icing to pipe holly berries.

Fill with a variety of sweets, chocolates, after-dinner mints, marzipan fruits or even little individual presents. Display the sleigh on a doily or wooden board.

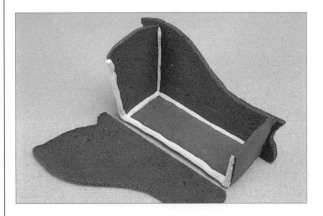

ASSEMBLING THE GINGERBREAD SLEIGH
Pipe a line of icing right around the edge of the three standing pieces and add the final panel. Remove any icing that has been squeezed from the joins.

CHRISTMAS AT THE POLE

Seals and icebergs, polar bears and Christmas presents complete a novelty cake which is very simple to decorate. The cake is baked in a dome-shaped tin (pan): a partially filled Dolly Varden, tiffin or bell tin (pan) is suitable, or half of a spherical Christmas pudding tin (pan) may be used. If you are really stuck, then use an ovenproof pudding basin.

2kg (4 lb) dome-shaped cake
750g (1½ lb) Marzipan (almond paste), see page 8
2kg (4 lb) Sugarpaste, see page 8
250g (8 oz) Pastillage, see page 10
125g (4 oz/½ cup) Royal Icing, see page 9
black, blue, red, pink, green and yellow paste
food colours
3 holly leaves, see page 15
about 1 tablespoons piping gel
EQUIPMENT
set of modelling tools
small glass jar or suitable container for setting
igloo tunnel
36cm (14 inch) oval cake board
no. 10 S-shaped crimper
large knife
1 cocktail stick (toothpick)
strand of covered wire or cotton
3.5cm (1½ inch) round cutter

Cover the cake with marzipan (almond paste) and sugarpaste. Cut the entrance tunnel in sugarpaste using the pattern on page 44 and lay this over a suitable jar as shown below. Then leave to dry overnight.

Set aside 250g (8 oz) sugarpaste to make the figures and cover the cake board with the remaining paste. Use the S-shaped crimper to crimp around the edge of the board. Place the cake towards the edge of the cake board, in order to leave room for the pastillage models,

and use the 3.5cm (1½ inch) round cutter to cut out a circle of paste, about 7.5cm (3 inch) away from the front of the igloo. Place the entrance tunnel on the igloo. Use the royal icing to rough ice the board.

Roll the white pastillage to a thickness of 2.5mm (⅛ inch) and use a large knife to cut out the icebergs following the pattern on pages 44 and 45. Leave the icebergs to dry overnight. Cut out a thin circle of pastillage to fit the hole in the paste covering the board; paint it mottled blue and put it in the fishing hole. Mix any remaining pastillage with the sugarpaste for modelling the figures following the methods shown on pages 16 and 17.

Use royal icing to conceal the join between the igloo and its entrance tunnel, which can be festooned with sugar icicles, holly leaves and berries. Place the figures in position. The eskimo on the left is fishing for presents through a hole in the ice. A cocktail stick (toothpick) and covered wire or cotton thread make up his fishing rod. Cover the blue circle with a small quantity of piping gel to give the impression that there is water in the hole.

---

1 **2**

1 Before the paste covering hardens, indent the lines. Use a scraper for horizontal lines, and a modelling tool for vertical lines. The entrance tunnel is dried over a glass jar.
2 The eskimo's legs are made from a U-shaped piece of red paste tapered at each end. The torso and hood are made from blue paste. The hands are formed like mittens. The wrists fit into the hollowed ends of each arm. Long strips of paste trim the clothing edges.

MERRY-MAKING ROBINS

These little creatures have become thoroughly involved with the festive spirit. I think that the conventional robin-on-a-log cake is in need of a fresh interpretation, and this particular cake appeals greatly to inveterate party-goers.

18cm (7 inch) round fruit cake
1kg (2 lb) Marzipan (almond paste), see page 8
red, dark brown, chestnut, black, Cornish cream and
green paste food colours
500g (1 lb/2 cups) Royal Icing, see page 9
icing (confectioners') sugar
125g (4 oz) Pastillage, see page 10
gold food paint
3 holly leaves, see page 15
EQUIPMENT
30cm (12 inch) round cake board
sieve ● paintbrushes
scriber ●fine-pointed scissors
modelling sticks or cocktail sticks (toothpicks)

🎄 Cover the cake with marzipan, reserving all the trimmings. Leave to dry for 1 – 2 days. Brush the top of the cake with boiled water or alcohol and follow step 1, below, for applying the top covering. Place it on the board and wrap a thick sausage of leftover marzipan from the top around the bottom edge. Colour 250g (8 oz/1 cup) royal icing dark brown and rough ice the side of the cake, texturing the wet icing with a fork to create the bark-like effect.

🎄 When the brown icing has dried, carefully rough ice the rest of the board with white royal icing. Thin the rest of the white icing with water until it has the consistency of thick cream and pour this over the top of the log to represent snow. Sprinkle the sides of the cake with a little sifted icing (confectioners') sugar.

🎄 Roll out a small rectangle of pastillage, then roll each end over a cocktail stick to form the scroll and set this aside to dry. Mix any scraps of marzipan with the rest of the pastillage and colour small amounts red, yellow and green. Divide the rest in half and colour one half light brown and the other half chestnut.

🎄 Make all the birds from similar pieces, following the patterns for the wings, tail and beaks on page 45, and step 2, below. Flatten a small amount of red paste on top of a walnut-sized piece of light-brown paste and roll together. Mark the bodies with a scriber and make tiny sausages, about 2.5cm (1 inch) long, for legs. Mould a pear-shaped head, then squeeze slightly to flatten the narrow end. Indent the eyes. Snip out a crown of feathers on the top and two feathers on the fattest part of the cheeks. Use the very small plastic modelling stick or cocktail stick (toothpick) to indent the feather pattern on the wings.

🎄 Fill the eye sockets with white royal icing and dry Paint the faces carefully so that their expressions are different. Paint the eyes with black food colour, so that two faces appear to be frowning and the others seem sleepy. Leave to dry before fitting the beaks which are folded diamond-shaped pieces of red and yellow paste.

🎄 The only parts not hardened before assembly are the birds' wings and tails which must be draped around the bodies and arranged differently for each bird. The champagne bottle is a piece of solid green paste, painted with black and gold food colour. Arrange the birds on the cake, adding the bottle, scroll and holly leaves.

1

2

1 To make the rings on the top of the cake, roll out some marzipan (almond paste) and paint it with food colour. Slice it into strips and roll them up tightly. Then trim the sides of the roll so that they are smooth. Slice a layer from the roll, lay it flat and roll it out until it is large enough to fit the top of the cake.
2 Making a robin: the pieces of paste, showing the stages in modelling the bird and marking its features, as described above.

CHRISTMAS BOOT

If, like the 'Old Woman who Lived in a Shoe' in the children's rhyme, you need a large Christmas cake, this one is entirely suitable. It is two cakes in fact, an oval one and a smaller round one which fits on one end to make the ankle and top of the boot.

25 x 18cm (10 x 7 inch) oval fruit cake
15cm (6 inch) round cake
1.25kg (2½ lb) Sugarpaste, see page 8
variety of modelled figures and toys, see pages 18 – 22
red paste food colour
750g (1½ lb) Marzipan (almond paste), see page 8
60ml (2 fl oz/¼ cup) sherry, brandy or rum
250g (8 oz/1 cup) Royal Icing, see page 9
gold dragees (nonpareils)
EQUIPMENT
36 x 25cm (14 x 10 inch) cake board
palette knife
paintbrush

Prepare the boot by cutting and assembling the cakes as shown below. Colour 750g (1½ lb) sugarpaste red. Reserve a little white sugarpaste, then use the remainder to model the toys and figures.

Cover the cake with a layer of marzipan (almond paste). Before the paste hardens, brush with sherry, brandy or rum, except for the hollow on the smaller section. Cover the boot with the red sugarpaste, using your hands to smooth the paste around the bulges. Tuck the bottom edge of the paste underneath the cake so that it has a rounded appearance. Cut a 15cm (6 inch) circle out of the red paste in the hollow. Brush this area with alcohol and replace the red paste with a circle of

white sugarpaste. Model a few holly berries from the remnants of red sugarpaste.

Use a palette knife to smooth a generous amount of royal icing around the top edge of the boot, then swirl it with a paintbrush into a bold pattern to represent the boot's fur lining. Leave this to dry. Add the figures and toys to the boot, with the holly berries and gold dragees (nonpareils).

The ankle of the boot is built up by fitting the 15cm (6 inch) round cake onto the end of the oval cake. Cut a cone-shaped hollow into the top of the round cake so that, when it has been iced, the toys and models will rest in it. Stick strips of marzipan to the cake with piping gel to create the wrinkles in the surface of the boot before applying the covering of marzipan.

MERRY CHRISTMAS CAKE

A strong design in bright and clear colours gives this bell-shaped cake a very festive feel. There are two forms of run-out used here: the design on the top is flooded directly onto the icing, while the trees and parcels arranged on the sides are flooded onto wax paper and attached to the cake later.

25 x 23cm (10 x 9inch) flat bell-shaped cake
750g (1½ lb) Marzipan (almond paste), see page 8
1.25kg (2½ lb) Sugarpaste, see page 8
500g (1 lb/2 cups) Royal Icing, see page 9
red, blue, green, yellow, pink and skintone paste
food colours
piping gel
3 holly leaves, see page 15
EQUIPMENT
36 x 33cm (14 x 13 inch) bell-shaped cake board
non-stick teflon-coated cloth or wax paper
nos. 1 and 0 piping tubes (tips)
piping bags
paintbrush
1 metre (40 inch) of 3mm (¼ inch) wide red ribbon

Cover the cake with marzipan (almond paste) and sugarpaste. Cover the board with sugarpaste and set both aside to dry separately. Place the cake on the board. It is important to plan the order of applying the icing before you begin. As you trace the pattern, see page 45, and transfer it to the cake top, give some thought to the different parts of the design and work out which sections to fill in first. It is best to start with those parts of the design which appear to be the most distant. Then, if there is any overlap between the icing on different sections, those parts which appear nearer overlap those further away. For the little girl in this picture, the arm and the stocking are closest, so they should be flooded after the main part of her gown. Follow the instructions on flooding on page 14. Start with the white sections, even if they do appear to be closer, or there is a risk of the red colour bleeding into the white.

The same principal applies when flooding the side pieces, which are made on a non-stick mat, so complete the tubs before you fill in the Christmas trees. Allow at least 24 hours for the designs to dry before releasing them and attaching them to the cake with royal icing.

The parcels on the stocking are flooded separately and attached with a little royal icing when completely dry. The toe and heel areas of the stocking are overpiped using a no. 1 piping tube (tip) and the buttons on the front of the gown are added using the same tube (tip). A little stiff white royal icing is added to the edges of the hat and gown, and roughened with a paintbrush. Paint the details of the hair and face outline using skintone food colour.

Pipe the greeting on the cake using a no. 1 piping tube (tip) and red royal icing of normal piping consistency. Finish the cake with a narrow ribbon around the bottom edge, attached with piping gel. Attach the three holly leaves on the top of the stocking after the parcels have been positioned and secure them with a dot of royal icing.

BURGUNDY CAKE

Elegant and classical best describe this burgundy-coloured Christmas celebration cake, with three slender candles which lend a touch of romance to the design.

20cm (8 inch) square cake
750 g (1½ lb) Marzipan (almond paste), see page 8
1kg (2 lb) Sugarpaste, see page 8, coloured deep pink
burgundy paste food colour
125g (4 oz/½ cup) Royal Icing, see page 9
gold dragees (nonpareils)

EQUIPMENT

28 cm (11 inch) square thin cake board
no. 9 holly leaf crimper
star and cone modelling tools
confectioners' glaze
set of holly leaf cutters
rose leave veiners
3 x 13 cm (5 inch) slim pink candles
piping bags
nos. 1 shell and 43 piping tubes (tips)
1.5 metres (1¾ yd) burgundy tartan ribbon

🌿 Cover a fruit cake with marzipan (almond paste) and leave to dry for 1 – 2 days. Then cover the cake with pink sugarpaste. Before the sugarpaste begins to harden, make a paper template to fit around the sides of the cake. Fold the template into eight and cut it into a curve across the top. Unfold the paper, then pin this scallop pattern around the cake and use it as a guide to position the holly leaf design. Impress the design in the soft paste using a crimper or a holly cutter. Use a star modelling tool to impress the central vein on each leaf and use the cone modelling tool to indent the holly berries between each leaf.

🌿 The leaves, parcels and the larger balls on the top of the cake are made from the scraps of paste left after covering the cake. Cut six 2.5cm (1 inch) cubes for the pink parcels, then colour the remaining paste deep burgundy. Roll four balls of paste the same size as the parcels and leave these to dry, then dip them in confectioners' glaze.

🌿 Make 16 large, 15 medium and 14 small holly leaves, see page 15. Mark their veins with rose leaf veiners and leave to dry. Paint the leaves with two layers of confectioners' glaze so that they have a high gloss.

🌿 Dampen the back of a piece of soft sugarpaste about the size of a golf ball and place it on the centre of the cake, flatten it slightly and insert the three candles into it. Using a no. 1 piping tube (tip) and burgundy royal icing, pipe the ribbons around the parcels and attach these and the glazed balls to the cake with royal icing. Push the tips of the holly leaves into the central ball of paste and leave to set.

🌿 Add a few gold dragees (nonpareils) to give the centrepiece extra sparkle. Finish the cake with a shell border around the base and a bow of ribbon.

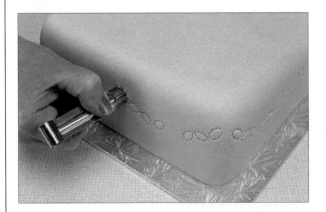

Embossing with crimping tools is a basic and simple technique for marking patterns. As well as this holly shape there are hearts, diamonds and scallops and they are available in widths from 1 – 3.5cm (½-1½ inch). Use them to press the pattern into soft sugarpaste coating.

HOLLY CAKE

Simplicity is the keynote of this sugarpaste-decorated cake which can be assembled in a matter of minutes once the pastillage pieces are dry. If preferred, royal icing may be used for the coating.

23cm (9 inch) round cake
1kg (2 lb) Marzipan (almond paste), see page 8
1.75kg (3½ lb) Sugarpaste, see page 8
185g (6 oz) Pastillage, see page 10
dark green and red paste food colour
red, yellow and blue dusting powders
125g (4oz/½ cup) Royal Icing, see page 9
cornflour (cornstarch)
EQUIPMENT
33cm (13 inch) round cake board
no. 5 piping tube (tip)
1 metre (40 inch) of 1cm (½ inch) wide
scarlet ribbon for board edging
12cm (4½ inch) long holly leaf cutter
clear corrugated P.V.C. sheeting
confectioners' glaze (optional)

Cover the cake with marzipan (almond paste) and set aside for 1 – 2 days. Coat the cake board with sugarpaste the day before covering the cake.

Colour about 155g (5 oz) of the pastillage dark green, make sure that it is mixed by thoroughly kneading for several minutes. Store this paste in a plastic bag and cut off just enough to make about two or three leaves at a time. Roll out the paste to a thickness of about 2mm (⅛ inch), which is perfect for most pastillage that is to be used flat or moulded into simple curves. Curve the leaves as shown below. Cut out 20 leaves: although you will only use about 15 on the cake it is wise to make a few extra in case of breakages. Leave in a dry, warm place for 24 hours.

The flame is made from white pastillage: using the same holly cutter, cut two leaves, then cut a 2 mm (⅛ inch) slot from the base up the centre of the leaf. This slot should be 5cm (2 inch) long and it should end about midway along the length of the leaf. Take the second leaf and cut a similar slot, this time cutting from the tip down to the middle of the leaf. Let the leaves dry flat for 24 hours, then colour them with red and yellow dusting powder to represent a flame as shown below. Dust just a touch of blue into the base of the flame. Slot the two leaves together.

Make the candle from a thick sausage of white sugarpaste, about 5cm (2 inch) high by 7.5cm (3 inch) wide. Wrap a layer of red sugarpaste around the outside. While the paste is soft, mould one end to a slight peak on one side. Form a depression in the centre. Indent a lip into one side of the candle for the wax to run out. Push the flame into the centre while the paste is soft.

Pipe a row of small shells around the base of the cake. When the holly leaves are dry, clean the edges with a sharp craft knife or emery board. Stick them to the cake using a dab of icing behind each one. Make holly berries by rolling small balls of red sugarpaste: you can make them shine by dipping them in confectioners' glaze and letting them dry. Use a little royal icing to stick three berries at the base of each leaf.

If you have any royal icing, run some down the candle to make the pool of wax, otherwise use soft sugarpaste and mould it to shape. Finally, glue the scarlet ribbon around the edge of the board.

1

2

1 Lightly dust the corrugated sheeting with cornflour. Lay the leaves along the ridges as soon as they are cut. Make sure that all the leaves take on the same curve.
2 Apply dusting powder to hardened paste using a fairly large brush. Stipple the colour on, working from the outside edge into the middle of the flower or leaf. Always work on a piece of kitchen roll or tissue as it is easier to clean up.

TEMPLATES

FOR *QUICK AND EASY* CAKES

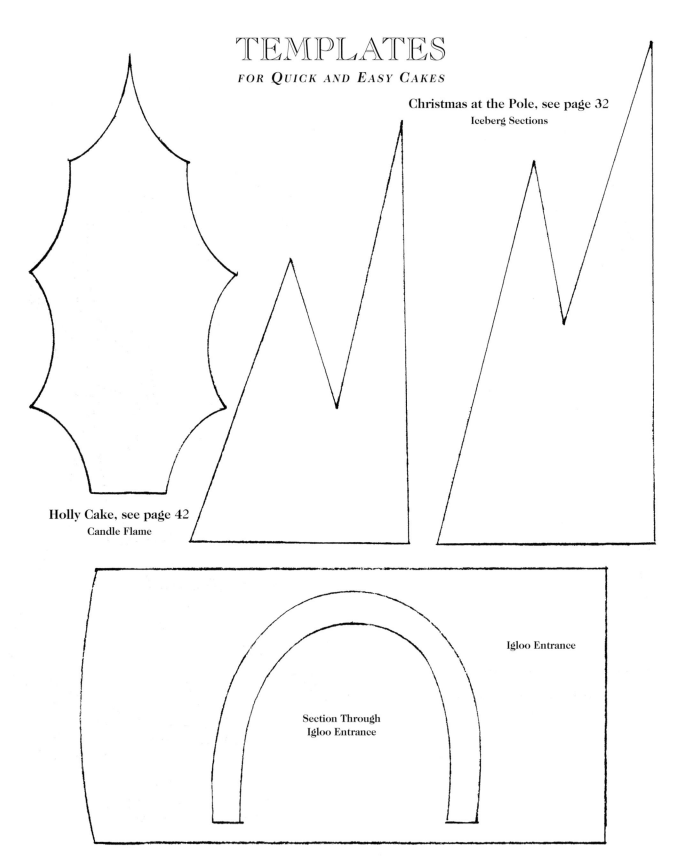

Christmas at the Pole, see page 32
Iceberg Sections

Holly Cake, see page 42
Candle Flame

Igloo Entrance

Section Through
Igloo Entrance

44

Merry-Making Robins, see page 34

Bird's Tail

Bird's Beak

Bird's Wings

Christmas at The Pole, see page 32
Iceberg Section

Merry Christmas Cake, see page 38
Run-out Design for Cake Top

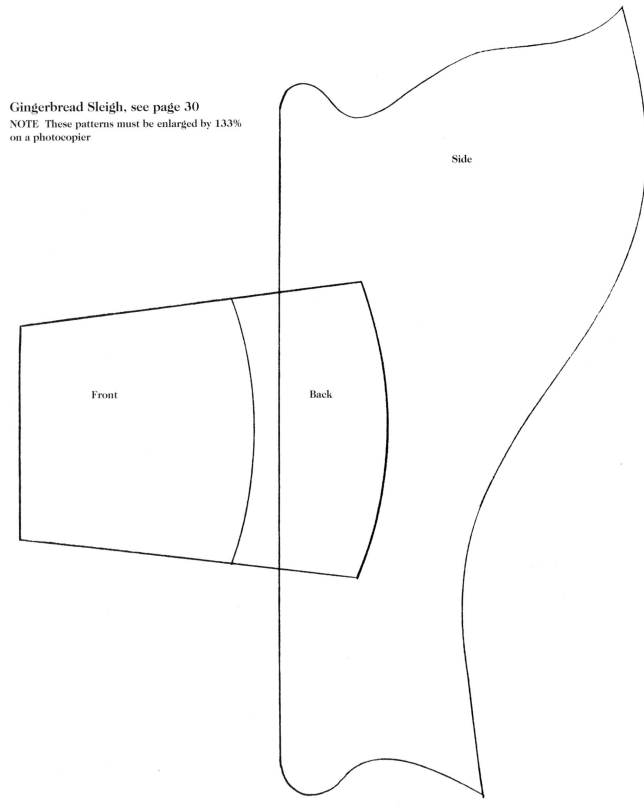

Gingerbread Sleigh, see page 30
NOTE These patterns must be enlarged by 133%
on a photocopier

Side

Front

Back

Santa Cake, see page 24

Moustache

Hat

Cuff and Boot
Trimmings

Boots

Beard

Gingerbread Sleigh, see page 30
NOTE This template must be enlarged by 133%
on a photocopier

Base

INDEX